Teenagers: Everyone Is NOT Doing It

D0167098

Teenagers:
Everyone Is NOT Doing It

Mike Long Talks to Teens About Sex

Mike Long

Jameson Books
Ottawa, Illinois

To Kathleen Sullivan of Project Reality, and to all those others who have worked tirelessly over the years to insure the highest standards and values for America's youth.

Cover photography by Paul Liggitt Photography, Durham, NC
Illustrations by David Griffith

Jameson books are available at special discounts for bulk purchases for sales promotions, premiums, fundraising or educational use. Special condensed or excerpted paperback editions can also be created to customer specifications.

For information or other requests please write:
  Jameson Books, Inc
  722 Columbus Street
  Ottawa, Illinois 61350
  815-434-7905 • FAX 815-434-7907
  E-mail 72557.3635@compuserve.com

Jameson Books titles are distributed to the book trade by LPC Group, 1436 West Randolph Street, Chicago, IL 60607. Bookstores should call 800-243-0138.

Individuals who wish to order by mail should call 800-426-1357.

ISBN 0-915463-87-3

Manufactured in the United States of America

10 9 8 7 6 5 4   / 05 04

Table of Contents

by Dean Smith

**Former Basketball Coach of the University
of North Carolina**

Many of the college athletes
I've coached have gone on
to become tremendously
successful. The ones who did—
like Michael Jordan—were able
to apply the same lessons they
learned while playing basketball
to situations they faced in other arenas.

When a player makes the right move on the basketball court it's almost always because he's practiced
and practiced that same move until it becomes almost
automatic. People who watch him during a game
think he makes a split-second decision that scores a
basket to win a game, when actually he's already made
that decision a hundred times in drill after drill. By
the time he gets in the game, the right moves come
naturally.

Making the right decisions about sex, drugs, alcohol, and other risky behaviors can come just as eas-
ily to kids if they've gone through the right drill. That's
what struck me about Mike Long the first time I heard
him speak: he teaches kids how to make the right
moves.

He's done it in personal appearances since 1986—
all over the country, to middle and high school

students, to college students, and to their teachers and parents. He's also done it in a video series that is sweeping the country.

And he does it in this book.

•

Everyone is NOT Doing It: Mike Long Talks to Teens About Sex

L inda and her best friend, Alice, are 17 years old, and both are virgins. They've talked about having sex with their boyfriends. But, for several reasons, neither girl believes she should take this serious step.

Some of their friends feel differently. Several have already had sex—or say they have—and are urging Linda to try it. "You two are the only ones who aren't doing it," they say. "Everyone thinks you're weird."

Both girls regularly watch several TV shows featuring teenagers—sitcoms and dramas—in which all the characters are sexually active. They've also noticed that movies made for teenagers paint the same picture—young people having sex without consequences or regrets.

The popular music they hear on the radio sends an even stronger implied message, as do many of the ads in magazines: Have sex! Be popular!

And in Health 201, their textbook leads them to believe it's okay to have sex as long as you use a condom.

In fact, everywhere they turn, Linda and Alice wonder if they *are* the only ones not doing it. And if that *really* makes them weird.

Lately, Linda's boyfriend, Kevin, has been pushing her as well. He's even hinted that if she doesn't love him enough to take this step, he may dump her.

Deep inside, Kevin also has reservations about having sex. But his friends are pressuring him, too, saying, "You've been going with Linda for almost a year now, and you two still haven't done it? What's wrong with you? Go for it! Be a man! Everyone else is doing it!"

Alice has an easier time. Her boyfriend, Ricky, says he understands her reasons for wanting to remain a virgin and has promised to respect her wishes. Sometimes, however, they both feel very strong physical desire and wonder if some night their feelings will carry them over the edge.

Unfortunately, their parents haven't been much help. Linda's mother tells her not to have sex—period. But when Linda wants to discuss the subject at greater length, her mother changes the subject.

Kevin's parents are divorced, and his father lives 500 miles away—in another state. Kevin doesn't feel comfortable talking to his mother about sex.

Alice's mother has spoken to her about the risks of having sex—pregnancy, disease, emotional trauma. "However, if you are going to do it anyway," she says, "then make certain you're protected. Better safe than sorry."

Ricky's parents have avoided the issue with him. His mother and father presume he knows what's right.

This Saturday night, Kevin's parents will be out of town, and the two couples are planning to spend the evening at Kevin's house—without adult supervision. Linda and Alice have talked about these plans and are worried.

Under these circumstances, can they control the situation? And can they control their own desires?

The simplest way for the two couples to respond to all these pressures is to remain firm, to continue to "just say no" to sex. But making sexual decisions is not that simple. Sex is a very complex experience, one that involves physical feelings, personal relationships, moral judgments, and social consequences.

To teenagers, the pressure to have sex often seems irresistible. They're torn, confused, uncertain of how they should react to a world that's constantly urging them to be sexually active. They need some direction, and they don't know where to turn.

If you know Linda and Alice and Kevin and Ricky, get them to read this book before Saturday. It may save them from a lifetime of pain and regret.

And if you see yourself in this picture—if you're trying to make sexual decisions and having a hard time—then read on for some real direction that will help you.

Part One

What's Going On Here?

Chapter One

Bad and Good News About Today's Teenagers

Our teenagers are out of control. They're all having sex. They're all into alcohol and drugs. They're all bringing weapons to school and killing each other in the streets. They're tearing down our society, and there's nothing we can do about it.

*H*ow many times have you heard adults say something like that? Probably almost as often as I have.

And maybe there's some truth in what they say. But that's by no means the whole story.

The most recent studies show a downward trend in teenage sexual activity, drug use, and violence. For example, the Centers for Disease Control report that between 1990 and 1995, the percentage of girls who had ever engaged in intercourse dropped to 50 percent and to 47.7 percent by 1997.[1] For boys, the figure dropped from 57.4 percent in 1991 to 48.8 percent in 1997.[2] This means that for the first time in decades, a majority of teenagers are not having sex.

These trends indicate a new sense of responsibility in your generation, and I tell people about it wherever I go and whenever I can. You've

Responsibility

proven that young people *can* change their behavior in positive ways and that bad trends can be reversed.

However, in order to do that, you have to be aware of the pitfalls you face in today's society—the many voices that keep telling you, "Everyone is doing it. What are you waiting for?" Wherever I go, teenagers identify the same pressures, and we'll take a look at these pressures in the next chapter.

Chapter Two

Top Ten List of Pressures on Teens to Have Sex

What pressures encourage you to have sex? If you're like the average teenager I've met while crisscrossing the country, you know they come from a variety of sources. Teens tell me they experience such pressures daily—and that in combination these influences are hard to resist.

So let's look at the Top Ten List of Pressures on Teenagers to Have Sex. And remember, I didn't make up this list. Teenagers just like you told me what forces have pushed them toward sexual activity.

1. Pressure from other teenagers

According to most teens, "peer pressure," as psychologists call it, is the single most important influence in the way they behave—and peer pressure is the most difficult to resist.

If you're a male, the guys may tell you that it's macho to have sex with as many girls as possible, that if you haven't had sex there's something wrong with you. You're a wimp. You're weird. You're a nerd. And if you say, "I don't believe in having sex before marriage," they tease you.

If you're a female, they may say

5

you're cold or scared or uncool. They say that everyone else is doing it, that there's something wrong with you if you're still a virgin.

However, at the same time, a girl knows that if she *does* have sex, others will find out about it—and some of them will call her a slut.

I sympathize with kids who want to be one of the "in-group." We all do. And often adults make the same choice that many teens make: They do things that are against their principles just so they can "fit it"—so they can belong to the right club, run with the right crowd. Small wonder teenagers are often tempted to make the same mistake.

2. Television

After school, most kids go home and plop in front of the television set. Some of them stay there until the evening meal, then return and watch until bedtime. Studies have repeatedly shown that the average teenager spends more time in front of the TV than in the classroom.

These days, daytime television is crowded with MTV and sexy soaps. And nighttime programming is full of explicit dramatic shows and sexually oriented sitcoms. Sitcoms in particular focus on sex because it's easy to get a cheap laugh from sexual antics. If the lines aren't really funny, audiences will laugh anyway—if only out of surprise and mild shock.

3. Movies

As you've undoubtedly found out, movies can be more explicit than television shows (though in recent years TV has been closing the gap).

The messages Hollywood sends out are loud and clear: Everyone's having sex, and there's nothing wrong with it.

The people who make these movies have run frequent surveys to determine who's coming to the theater and buying tickets. Over the years, teens have made up a larger and larger portion of the audience.

So Hollywood began making films specifically tailored to kids your age.

These films should give you a good idea of what Hollywood thinks about you. You like repeated sex scenes, sometimes interrupted by scenes of gruesome violence—the more graphic the better. And you don't really care if the movie contains anything else of interest or value—like an imaginative plot or complex characters.

Too many teenagers believe the **Great Hollywood Sex Myth**—that they can have casual sex and enjoy the experience without regrets or disastrous consequences.

If they see two good-looking teenagers having sex on the screen without problems or regrets, they get the message:

◆ It's okay
◆ It's pleasurable.
◆ It's safe.
◆ *Everyone is doing it!*

4. Tapes, CDs, music videos

If anything, today's music sends out more graphic and more dangerous messages than TV or the movies.

Rock singers and gangsta rappers glorify casual sex, rape, the occult, the infliction of pain, and even murder. They also use obscene language. Their purpose is to be more shocking and explicit than the last group and therefore more exciting.

The average parent can't understand the lyrics of these songs. However, they allow their teenagers to buy them and listen to them for hours on end. Most teens listen through headphones because they don't want their parents to hear these lyrics.

"But wait a minute, Mike," teenagers tell me, "I don't listen to the music for the lyrics ... I listen for the beat."

I like a good beat, too.

But you can have the same beat with a different message. And it's impossible for teens to listen to these lyrics over and over without being affected by the words and their meaning. If you think the music you listen to has no effect on you, then consider the number of teens you know who want to look, act, talk, and be just like their favorite music group. The truth is, teens *are* affected— more than they sometimes realize. Also, music videos are full of highly explicit sexual images. Like the songs they accompany, they are calculated to excite teenagers, who are just about the only ones who buy them. Scientific studies show that repeated exposure to the sexual images in pornography warps your imagination and stunts your sexual development.

Yet teenagers are watching explicit sexual images almost daily when they play and replay these music videos. And no one can say for sure how badly it has damaged their ability to think clearly about sex.

5. Books and magazines

An increasing number of books and magazines are devoted exclusively to the exploitation of sex.

Many of the most popular novelists do little more than string together a series of highly explicit sex scenes with little emphasis on plot and less on character. Some of these write fiction exclusively for the teenage market.

Sexually oriented magazines sold at newsstands and convenience stores range from graphic hard-core pornography (available to teenagers and adults alike) to publications specifically designed to appeal to teens. Even comic books—once harmless distractions for younger children—portray almost every kind of sexual activity.

6. Advertising

Teenagers are inclined to be more perceptive about advertising than many adults. Maybe it's because they bring a fresh point of view to the ads they see in magazines, newspapers, and on television.

Whatever the reason, they tell me that much of the advertising geared to the teen market is sexual in content. Many also recognize the false message that advertisers are sending:

◆ "If you buy a particular brand of jeans you'll be sexier and appeal to the good-looking girls."
◆ "Drink a particular cola and you'll soon be lying in bed with a hunk."
◆ "Buy skimpy underwear from a particular mall shop, and you'll be a sexual star."

Some teenagers recognize the lie behind such advertising, but many do not. And regardless of whether or not these ads persuade you to buy certain products, they still send the same old message: "Everyone's obsessed with sex. Everyone's doing it."

The bottom line is, all these advertisers are trying to do is play on your sexual nature (like everyone else, you're a sexual being) in order to make you believe that if you buy their product, you will become the person they show you in the ad. It's a lie—though one that often fools young people and adults as well.

7. Sex ed programs at school

A number of teenagers have told me that the sex education programs in their schools sometimes encourage them to be sexually active. I've examined some of these programs, and you know something? *These teens are right!* Some sex ed programs *do* send a mixed message to young people. And others go even further.

They actually teach middle school and high school students how to have sex and encourage them to engage in sexual behavior— as long as they do it "safely."

When I say some sex ed programs send a "mixed message," I mean that they may recommend abstinence as one method of avoiding pregnancy and disease, then tell teens they can protect themselves from these unwanted consequences simply by using a condom.

I will say more about this approach later. However, one thing should be clear: If you tell people not to do something, then let them know you think they're going to do it anyway, they aren't going to take the first part of your message very seriously.

Imagine saying to teens, "Now we don't want you to bring guns to school; but if you do, make sure the safety is on." What would the teens conclude?

It's okay to bring guns to school.

If someone is telling you it's okay to have sex, and actually showing you how to enjoy various sexual experiences while "protecting" yourself, it's hard to listen to the voices that tell you why it makes sense to abstain from sex and all the benefits you will enjoy as a teenager in doing so.

8. Family members and other adults

I was surprised when some teenagers told me that adult family members had encouraged them to have sex—if not in actual words, then by example.

For one thing, the number of single-parent families

has increased alarmingly over the past four decades. As a consequence, many mothers and fathers are dating again, and some bring home their dates to spend the night—or come home themselves at 9:00 the next morning. Also, there are a number of moms and dads in two-parent families who misbehave sexually.

Such misbehavior is extremely disturbing to children of all ages, but it can be particularly hard on teenagers, who understand what's going on.

It's difficult for parents to command respect if they say, "Don't have sex. It's a mistake," and then set a poor example by their own sexual conduct.

Friends of parents often set a bad example as well. Many teenagers have shared these concerns with me:

◆ They learn that Bob and Susie, the couple next door, aren't married.
◆ They listen as Uncle Jack brags about his new live-in girl friend.
◆ Mom's old college roommate comes for a two-day visit. She brings her boyfriend, and they share the guest room.
◆ And dad keeps copies of *Playboy, Penthouse,* and *Hustler* around the house—sending a message to his kids that his interest in sex isn't necessarily confined to mom.

Small wonder that kids who tell me these things also say they have a hard time listening to lectures from adults who behave in such a way.

"Do as I say, not as I do" isn't a very solid platform on which to stand in advising teenagers about sex.

9. Internet

More and more teens are logging on the Internet—and in many instances, their parents don't know how to turn a computer on, much less surf the web to discover what's out there. The result: a new world to explore and a new freedom from parental supervision.

But cyberspace can be dangerous. A huge proportion of websites are devoted to pornography and highly charged sexual conversation. Even when you're not looking for sex, it comes looking for you.

One father told me that he allowed his 12- and 13-year-old children to have their own website only after he'd installed a block to prevent them from accessing porn sites. However, as soon as the teens were online, they began to receive e-mail messages from porn merchants—filled with sexually graphic language and unblocked e-mail addresses where they could link up with sex partners. There was no way to prevent this invasion of the home.

In fact, the Internet offers the most explicit sexual images available in our culture, much of it sensational and even brutal. The Worldwide Web has become a chief method of soliciting sexual partners. Sick adults are preying on minors—engaging them in sex talk and arranging secret meetings. And more and more teenagers are discovering these sexually explicit sites.

10. An inner desire to be loved

This pressure is different from the others because it comes from *within* rather than from *without*.

Over the past several decades, the traditional family has become more and more unstable; and as a consequence, more and more children are being raised in troubled homes.

In many cases, single mothers and fathers are doing a terrific job. They set a good example for their teenagers. They talk to their teens about the dangers of drugs, alcohol, and sex. And they provide sound reasons for avoiding these dangers. They deserve more credit than they receive.

However, huge numbers of children are without a father or mother to provide that extra measure of love and reassurance that we all need.

As a consequence, there are some teenagers who seek sex as a means of receiving the warmth and affection they have missed at home.

And some girls even try to become pregnant so they can have another human being who loves them—and whom they can love. Such girls can't be persuaded to avoid sex by warning them that they might become pregnant. That's their purpose in becoming sexually active.

These, then, are what teenagers themselves regard as the Top Ten Pressures to Have Sex. You may be able to think of a few more, but ten is surely enough to remind us that we live in a "sex-charged" society—

full of problems and temptations that earlier genera-
tions never had to face.

I believe teenagers today are coping pretty well
with the pressures they're under, though I think we
can all do a lot better.

In order to deal with such pressures, however,
teens need clear direction from all segments of our
society. When you analyze these pressures carefully,
you may begin to see them in a different light.

We'll begin to do that in the next chapter.

Chapter Three

Peer Pressure

"*P*eer pressure" is an expression you probably know and use. Though it was invented by psychologists for use in scholarly discussions, the phrase has found its way into everyday speech. When I ask teenagers, "What's the biggest problem you face in abstaining from sex, drugs, and other risky behavior?" they often say "peer pressure," rather than "other teens" or "pressure from my friends."

So let's talk about peer pressure.

It's interesting to note that in a society where young people are supposed to be freer and more self-sufficient, everyone still wants to run with the rest of the crowd—so much so that they'll take big risks just to avoid feeling "different."

There's nothing wrong with wanting to fit in with the group. Unlike butterflies and snakes, human beings thrive in society and wither away in isolation.

In fact, one of life's great lessons is learning to control your own ego in order to get along with other people.

One way of "getting along" is to "go along"—to adopt the same rules and customs that society follows. You eat mashed potatoes with a fork, not with your fingers. You share with others. You drive on the proper side of the road and obey the traffic lights.

If everyone didn't behave exactly the same way in traffic, no one could drive down the street in safety.

But suppose the particular society you live in has bad habits and engages in dangerous practices? Do you want to "go along" with such people just to "get along"?

Of course not.

So do you just resign from society and go your separate way?

You don't want to do that either, do you?

That's the dilemma teenagers face today.

Society encourages you to have sex, use drugs, and carry weapons. At least *some* elements of society push you in that direction, while too often the rest stand by silently.

Here are some of the things teenagers say about peer pressure:

"I don't want to have sex, but my girlfriend keeps telling me to go ahead and try it, that I'll be thought of as a tease if I don't."

"They tell me I'm the only guy in the group who doesn't drink and hasn't had sex. They say I'm a nerd. This girl came up to me at a party the other night and kidded me about it. She said she wanted to have sex with me, but then she laughed. I could see that everyone else was watching us, so I guess they were in on the joke."

"It's hard to take the teasing. I'm not sure how long I can hold out. And my boyfriend is pressuring me too. What can I do about it?"

First, let me remind you that, according to that U.S. government study I've already cited, fewer than 50 percent of today's teenagers have had sex—and only half that many have had sex more than once. That figure may change next year, but not by much—and it might drop even lower. So a majority of teenagers *aren't* having sex.

"But wait a minute, Mr. Long," you're probably saying, "most of the kids I know have already had sex, and that's the group I hang out with."

Maybe they've had sex, and maybe they haven't. People lie a lot about sex—both ways. They say they *haven't* when they *have*—and they say they *have* when they *haven't*. So you can never be sure, can you?

But so what if they have?

Ask yourself this question, "If everyone in the group was playing Russian roulette with a loaded pistol, would you play too?" You see, it isn't always in your best interest to say, "Just because everyone's doing it, I have to do it too."

In the case of risky behavior, ask yourself, "What is best for *me?*"—and that's an entirely different question from "What is everyone else doing?"

If everyone's wearing green to school on St. Patrick's Day, then maybe you should consider wearing green as well, just to join in the group fun.

If everyone's having sex and risking pregnancy, STDs, and an emotional breakdown, then there's no reason for you to risk your future just because they're willing to risk theirs.

Of course, the most difficult kind of peer pressure to resist is the pressure brought by a girlfriend or boyfriend to have sex. Read these letters that I've received from teens and you'll see what I mean.

Here's a typical comment—the kind I get all the time from teenage girls who are sorry they had sex.

"Hi! I just watched some of your videos with my grandma. I just want to say thank you. Recently I messed up and let an older guy, who I thought really cared about me, take away my virginity. He knew all the right things to say. And drugs and alcohol played a big part in my decision.

"But your tapes helped me realize that I can change even though I messed up. And I made a promise to myself tonight that I will not mess around with drugs, alcohol, or sex, so that my drive for pleasure will stay down. I am also committing to stop smoking cigarettes. Thank you again. What you are doing is really awesome. Keep up the good work, Mr. Long."

The following is a message from an Ohio girl who regrets her earlier mistake and is frustrated because her friends won't listen to her warning.

"I just wanted you to know that I believe in what you are saying. I only wish I had heard your views before I decided to have sex. I thought I was in love, but now I realize it was more infatuation than anything.

"I try to tell my younger friends to wait, but they look at me like I was a hypocrite. All I can do is try."

A teenaged girl from North Carolina sent me this message, which mirrors her own confusion and also the confusion of millions like her.

"I saw your video in school, and, well, I guess it confused me. I don't know why. Well, I guess I do, but I don't.

"Anyway, I like this guy so-o-o much, and he feels the same about me. He lives six hours away—and, well, I'm moving soon, so he'll live 14 hours away then.

"And we talk everyday for hours on end. Well, we talk about sex a lot; and when he comes home in two weeks, we were thinking about having sex. But I don't know what to do.

"I want to [have sex], and it's something I've wanted to do for a long time with him, but at the same time I'm scared. No matter what happens, I know he'll be by my side, because we've discussed that—and it will be his first time too. Well, I just feel comfortable writing you with my so-called problem."

If you read between the lines, you'll understand that this girl had already decided to have sex with her boy friend but was never completely comfortable with her decision ("... at the same time I'm scared."). After hearing what I had to say, she was even more reluctant.

While she devoted much of her message to her strong desire to have sex with her boyfriend, she closed by putting her "problem" in my lap. So she really wanted me to tell her why she *shouldn't* take this step.

In addition to the usual reasons why *all* teenagers should abstain from sex, I also spotted additional complications in her case. For example, she wrote that "I know he'll be by my side, because we've discussed that...." Yet she also gave as one reason to have sex the fact that they would soon be living *14 hours apart*— she with her family, he with his.

So how could he possibly "be by her side" if, for example, she got pregnant?

Would he leave his family and move in with her parents just to "be by her side"?

21

When they discussed this possibility, did they consult both sets of parents? Obviously not.

Or would he drop out of school, get a job at a fast-food restaurant, and ask her to marry him?

The chances are that if she were to get pregnant, she and her parents would deal with the problem while he remained 14 hours away—perhaps worried about her situation, perhaps not. Distance can sometimes trick your conscience into forgetting responsibility. As the old saying goes, "Out of sight, out of mind."

But even if they lived in the same town, a teenaged guy can do little to solve the many problems that an out-of-wedlock pregnancy can pose. Parents generally have to make all the decisions, pay all the medical bills, and deal with the emotional consequences of sexual mistakes by teenagers.

So it isn't really fair for teenagers to think they have a right to decide whether or not to have sex. Not if someone else has to pay the price along with them.

It's easy for me to analyze this girl's situation—exploring all the angles of a situation and raising legitimate objections. I'm not in love with the guy.

But if you think you're in love, it's hard to be so analytical and objective.

So is there any way the three girls who wrote those letters could have determined whether the boy in question really loved them?

Yes, there *is* a way, as you'll see in Chapter Nine.

Meanwhile, let's look at the other major pressure on teenagers to have sex—the media.

Chapter Four

TV, Movies, and Music

I'd like to say a little more about the entertainment industry, since it wields such a strong influence on all our lives. Promoters in the entertainment industry make billions of dollars each year by pushing sexually oriented movies, TV programs, music videos, and recordings on teenagers like you. Many of these productions feature teenaged characters who have sex and enjoy every moment of it—and nobody is ever disappointed, gets pregnant, contracts a sexually transmitted disease, or loses the respect of friends and family.

The images you see on the screen or hear on your CD player are calculated to excite you, to make you think about sex more than you already do. Because as soon as you see that movie or listen to that song, they have more sex to sell you.

You are the most interesting person in the world to these sex merchants.

They run market surveys to see what will turn you on.

They want to know what magazines you read; what you think about your parents; and, above all, how much money you spend each week.

A long time ago, the sex merchants discovered an interesting fact about you: *You have more money to spend on entertainment than many adults.*

When law enforcement officers asked master criminal Willie Sutton why he robbed banks, he replied with a grin, "Because that's where the money is."

And that's why the Hollywood crowd goes after the teen market—*because that's where the money is.*

As soon as they made this discovery, the producers of movies, TV sitcoms, and music reinvented their product to appeal to you. (If you don't believe that, watch a classic movie channel that shows films from the 1930s, 1940s, and 1950s. You'll find no nudity, no explicit scenes, and no glorification of casual sex.)

However, in all the market research they conducted, there's one question they didn't ask: What does a steady diet of sexually explicit entertainment do to teens?

Or, to break the question down into several parts:

- Are teens healthier and happier because they watch sex movies and sex videos and listen to sex songs?
- Are they more likely to stay out of trouble?
- Do they get along better with their parents as a result?
- Do they treat each other with greater consideration, or are they more likely to use each other?
- Are they getting a realistic picture of sex and love and relationships when they see a Hollywood movie or a TV sitcom?

You know why the sex merchants didn't attempt to find an answer to those questions?

Because they weren't interested in the answers.

They didn't care what effect their products were having on you.

They just wanted your money.

However, the answers to those questions should be extremely important to you, since your happiness and your relationships with others are at stake.

I'm going to give you some straight answers in a minute. First, however, remember this: You didn't ask Hollywood to come after your money any more than a bank asks to be robbed. The sex merchants made all the moves.

And you needn't feel guilty about being interested in sex.

So am I. So is everyone else. We are sexual beings. We were made that way.

In fact, some of the greatest works of literature are about sex—from Homer to Shakespeare to Hawthorne. There's nothing wrong with talking about sex or making movies about sex or singing songs about sex. Love stories and love songs have existed throughout history.

It's *how* we talk about sex, *how* we depict it, *what* we think and say about it that distinguishes what's normal and healthy from what's vulgar or dishonest or dangerous.

So let me begin the straight talk by telling you this: The view of sex promoted in films, on TV, and in popular music is a deliberately falsified picture— the **Great Hollywood Sex Myth.**

Here are several of the ingredients of that myth and the contrasting reality:

Myth: Sex is fun and always pleasurable, even when casual. Both the guy and the girl find the experience exciting and completely satisfying.

Reality: Contrary to what Hollywood tells you, sex is not "fun." Ping Pong is fun. A carnival ride is fun. Sex is in an entirely different category. When engaged in under proper circumstances, it's *better* than fun—more complex, more soul-shaking, more uplifting. At the same time, on the screen, you never see the pain, the humiliation, the frustration, the embarrassment that too often come with sex between teenagers who aren't ready for the experience and the emotional consequences.

Myth: Sex is something you can share with anyone you find attractive, whether you've known your partner for a year or just met at a party.

Reality Sex between people who hardly know each other is usually unsatisfying, particularly for the girl. Real sex is a highly intimate union of two committed people, not a fumbling experiment with someone you've just met. Many married couples achieve a satisfying sex life only after they've lived together for a while, becoming accustomed to each other, knowing they can depend on each other. A happy sex life is something you have to earn over a period of time; it's not achieved in a single night by two teenagers in the back seat of an automobile.

Myth: After a movie couple enjoys sex, neither one feels guilty or used. Both are happy with the experience, their partner, and themselves.

Reality: Too often teenagers feel guilt and self-loathing after they've had sex, particularly for the first time. These are feelings you can't predict. After building up their expectations, many girls are terribly disappointed and even revolted by the experience. But in a Hollywood film, few girls cry themselves to sleep after consenting to have sex. Often after a real first sex experience, guys likewise have the feeling they've made a big mistake. (In fact, they can sometimes carry emotions far deeper than the girl's; but it's not macho to communicate these emotions if you're a teenage male today, so they build and build inside until, in some cases, they explode.)

 Myth: There are almost never unwanted consequences of Hollywood sex—no pregnancies, no sexually transmitted diseases, no aching emotional regrets.

Reality: Teenage girls get pregnant all the time, and almost four million teenagers contract one or more sexually transmitted diseases every year. (Has James Bond ever gotten a girl pregnant or contracted syphilis?)

 Myth: Having casual sex as a teenager won't affect your relationship with the person you marry, so enjoy yourself while you're young.

27

Reality: You never know whom you'll want to marry. The odds are overwhelming that it won't be the person you're dating now. Maybe that man or woman will regard virginity as an important indicator of character, and maybe, if you've been sexually active, he or she will find out. (If you've been pregnant or had a sexually transmitted disease, your chances of marrying such a person may be even slimmer.)

Myth: Parents, older family members, and clergy don't understand the sexual "needs" of teenagers because they don't feel those urges themselves and because they've forgotten what it was like to be young.

Reality: In Hollywood films, parents and clergy are morons, ogres, and hypocrites, always meddling in the lives of young people in love, unable to sympathize with the desires the lovers feel because they've never had such urges themselves or else have forgotten how it felt. This, too, is untrue. Most parents know exactly how teenagers feel, which is why they watch their children carefully, just the way their parents watched them. And clergy—who counsel members of their congregation daily and have heard a hundred sad stories—probably know more about sex than Hollywood scriptwriters. It's because they understand what sex is really all about that sensible parents and clergy advise young people to abstain from sex until marriage.

THE GREAT **HOLLYWOOD** *SEX MYTH*

I may have left out a few characteristics, but these are the important ingredients of the **Great Hollywood Sex Myth,** the sugar-coated lies that bring in the bucks of gullible teenagers.

And when you're in the theater watching a good-looking actor and actress play out this myth, it's very, very convincing. You can see yourself in that picture, and the thought is exciting.

Moved by such fantasies, too many young people end up as single mothers, prison inmates, alcoholics, drug addicts, and even corpses.

And what does the Hollywood crowd say about this?

Privately, they tell each other: "If teenagers see our movies or hear our records and go out and ruin their lives, it's not our fault. We're just reflecting society as it is today." And then they laugh all the way to the bank.

In this respect, movie, TV, and record producers are like drug dealers. They go after teenagers, because teenagers have money to spend—and they don't care if teens' lives are ruined or they end up dead in the street. If you didn't have money, they wouldn't give you the time of day. Because you have money, they'll exploit you any way they can.

Publicly, however, they say exactly what the

29

tobacco companies said: "There's no proof that our product harms children."

Oh, yeah? Here's what the studies show:

◆ In a publication called *Sex and the Mass Media,* the Kaiser Family Foundation reported that the media's "'love affair with sex and romance" promotes irresponsible sexual behavior among young people and is a measurable factor in teen pregnancy.[2]

◆ George Comerci, president of the American Academy of Pediatrics, stated: "In terms of modeling behavior, the older child particularly will repeat what he or she sees on TV, while the adolescent develops a personal attitude about the life and [the] world he or she lives in as a result of what they're seeing on television."[3]

And many more studies have come to the same conclusion. In the face of such evidence, however, the Hollywood crowd continues to deny that movies affect their audiences adversely.

Here's what movie critic Michael Medved had to say about such denials in his book *Hollywood vs. America: Popular Culture and the War on Traditional Values:*

The mighty mechanism of commercial television is based entirely on the premise that broadcast advertising can alter the buying behavior of a significant segment of the huge viewing audience.

It is the height of hypocrisy that the same network executives who accept and demand this lavish payment for the briefest moments of broadcast advertising try to convince us that all their many hours of programming do nothing to change the attitudes of the audience. In short, they have adopted the outrageously illogical assumption that a sixty second commercial makes a more significant impression than a sixty minute sitcom.[4]

I could give you more examples, but you get the point.

Hollywood sex merchants aren't the only people who have been less than honest with you. In the next chapter, we'll look at some sex education programs.

Chapter Five

Facts Your Sex Ed Textbook May Not Tell You

*J*ust as Hollywood hides the fact that ordinary people who wait until marriage are probably having better sex than Hollywood movie stars, so do some sex educators hide the fact that "safe sex" isn't really safe.

Recently, the Institute for Youth Development—a non-profit organization interested in the welfare of young people—brought together a number of teenagers to discuss their perception of their own lives and the world they live in. When the topic got around to sex education, several members of the two focus groups complained about the message they were receiving at school. While all students didn't encounter this problem, some teens said that so-called prevention programs actually encourage irresponsible sexual behavior.

One girl put it this way:

> "They give us condoms all of the time at our middle school. They give them to us like they're candy. You know it's like, 'We know you're not going to have sex, but if you do, here's a condom.' It's like they don't care as long as you don't come to their school pregnant. What they expect from us isn't clear."[5]

The courses about which these students complained send out a dangerous and misleading message:

"It's okay to have sex as long as you use a condom. You'll have a great time and you can protect yourself from unwanted consequences."

This is untrue. So just in case you haven't heard the facts, let me tell you about condoms and STD's.

Condoms

Here are three facts about condoms. They come from studies and reports issued by the U.S. government.[6]

Fact 1—The pregnancy rate among teenage girls whose partners use condoms is 16% to 18%. What exactly does this mean?

It means that, during a one-year period, 16 of every 100 sexually active girls who depend on condoms to prevent pregnancy *will get pregnant anyway.*

Do you think those are good odds?

Would you fly on an airline if you knew that 16 of every 100 planes they send up will crash within a year?

Fact 2—Condoms don't effectively prevent the spread of AIDS.

Many years ago, the U.S. Department of Health and Human Services funded a study in Los Angeles to see if the use of condoms would prevent the spread of the HIV virus. After a few months, it canceled the study. Why? Because too many of the condom users were becoming infected with AIDS.[7] Other such studies have produced similar results.

Fact 3—Despite widespread media reports to the contrary, condom use is not responsible for a recent drop in the rate of teenage pregnancy.

It's true that more couples are using condoms than ever before. It's also true that teenage pregnancy has recently decreased. However, the use of contraceptives *overall* has declined—including the pill, the most effective contraceptive of all. Let's analyze this. A less effective method of contraception (condoms) is up, but a more effective method (the pill) is down even more. How can this lead to reduced pregnancy?

It can't. It didn't.

Teenage pregnancy has declined *because fewer teens are having sex*. As I've noted elsewhere, according to the latest Centers for Disease Control figures, for the first time in many years, fewer than 50 percent of teenagers have tried sexual intercourse even once.

In 1998, the Kaiser Family Foundation's *National Survey of Teens* documented this new commitment to virginity. According to the Kaiser report, almost half of teenagers today have consciously chosen to remain virgins. Fully 44 percent of teens aged 13 to 18 say they have decided to delay intercourse and 74 percent of these say their fellow teens support this choice.[8]

As you've often heard, it's true that using condoms can reduce the risk of getting pregnant or catching a sexually transmitted disease. But when teenagers are so determined to have sex that they allow their emotions to outrun their reason, they often forget the sex educator's advice to use a condom. If you'll break society's rules about having sex outside of marriage, you'll probably find it even easier to ignore warnings about using a condom.

Because condom use has been emphasized in sex ed courses, in brochures handed out at school, in U.S. government literature, and in television ads, the more people hear such messages, the less they really listen to them.

Let me tell you a true story to illustrate what I mean.

A sex educator in one of the southern states became well known for her explicit courses about "human sexuality" and for her advice to high schools students to have sex if you want to, but use a condom. She was regarded as one of the most effective promoters of "safe sex" in her state.

So her admirers were shocked to read in the newspaper one day that she had been killed in an automobile accident. She'd been driving in rainy weather; and while rounding a corner, she had skidded. She was thrown from the car.

Had she been wearing a seat belt, she might not have died. And you know something? When she had her accident, she'd just driven past a sign that read: BUCKLE UP—IT'S A LAW WE CAN LIVE WITH.

She'd probably passed that sign hundreds of times—so many that the words no longer made an impression on her. Yet she believed that if you told teenagers to use condoms enough times, they'd get the message and practice what she called "safe sex."

Was she moving too fast when she

rounded that curve? Surely. She was violating the speed limit—breaking the rules imposed by society—and, at the same time, she didn't protect herself against the consequences of her speed-limit violation.

Don't make the same mistake. Don't believe you can have sex and protect yourself with a condom every time. The day will come when you'll be taking a corner so fast that you'll forget to use the safety device—or tell yourself, "I can take a chance just this once." And if you get away with it, you'll be tempted to try again.

Besides, remember that, like condoms, seat belts don't always protect you in the event of an automobile accident. Plenty of people are killed every year while wearing seat belts, just as plenty of pregnancies occur while condoms are in use. It's better to drive slowly—and to avoid sex before you're married and ready for the experience.

Sexually Transmitted Diseases (STDs)

Many sex education programs that leave nothing to the imagination where sex acts are concerned ignore the danger of sexually transmitted diseases.

I believe you should see the whole picture before you make a decision about becoming sexually active. So I'm going to give you a few facts about STDs you may not have gotten in sex ed.

◆ *Syphilis.* Over one million teenagers (ages 15 to 18) were infected last year with this dangerous and potentially fatal disease, which can eventually drive you insane.

◆ *Gonorrhea.* This highly painful disease is all too

common among teenagers and can affect your throat, your joints, and other portions of your body, as well as your sexual organs.

◆ *Genital Herpes.* This increasingly common sexually transmitted disease is caused in most cases by a virus called herpes simplex virus, type 2. Its symptoms are genital vesicles that evolve into painful ulcers.

◆ *Chlamydia.* Symptoms may include painful inflammation of the urinary tract and the vagina (in women) and pain in the pelvic area, the lower abdomen, and the groin. In women, lack of treatment can lead to an inability to have children.

◆ *Acquired Immune Deficiency Syndrome (AIDS).* The most deadly STD of all, AIDS was unknown until the 1980s, when it suddenly appeared in the homosexual community, then spread to the heterosexual community and to drug users who shared needles.

The HIV virus attacks your immune system; and, as a consequence, you contract a series of other diseases, several of which can cause death.

Recently, doctors have learned to prolong the lives of HIV-positive patients through drug treatment, but thus far no one has found a cure, despite the fact that AIDS research has received more funding than any other disease.

◆ *HPV—Genital Warts.* Genital warts are transmitted from skin to skin, so condoms don't offer protection. These growths are a leading cause of cervical cancer among women.

And there are 30 additional STDs you can contract, just by having sex *once*.

To avoid these threatening diseases, sensible teenagers decide to abstain from sex until marriage and to marry someone who's made the same intelligent and healthy decision.

Again, it's so simple.

But unthinking youngsters are forever telling themselves, "I'm in love and my boyfriend (or girlfriend) is strong and healthy. So why worry about disease?"

Unfortunately, all of these diseases can have a dormant stage during which no symptoms exist. In fact, some young people go around carrying the AIDS virus for months, even years, and never know it. And during that period, they can infect every sexual partner. Where syphilis and AIDS are concerned, the adage "looks can be deceiving" is chillingly true.

These, then, are some facts you need to know about condoms and STDs if you're pressured to become sexually active.

So don't make the mistake of believing the cheery propaganda about condoms.

Here's what a 17-year-old boy in Kalamazoo, Michigan, told me: "Mr. Long, I thought I was being responsible. I thought I was being safe. I thought I was being mature. I used a condom, just like they taught me in school. Why am I a father now?"

Part Two

Taking Charge
of Your Own Sexuality

Chapter Six

The Power to Decide

*I*n some ways, human beings are powerless.

As Mark Twain once wrote, "Everybody talks about the weather, but nobody does anything about it."

That's because we don't have the power to control the elements.

We can't prevent tornados or hurricanes—or even rain on the day of the Big Game. The best we can do is find a safe shelter or take an umbrella to the stadium.

But, unless we're mentally disturbed, we do have power over our own behavior—the power to decide whether we will engage in certain acts.

And that includes whether or not we will have sex.

Some commentators on adolescent behavior claim that teenagers simply can't control their "raging hormones," that—unlike adults—they are absolute slaves to their sexual appetites. That's just like saying teenagers are nothing more than animals.

You know that isn't true.

And, after talking with teens about this subject since the 1980s, I also know it isn't true. When I travel around the country, kids from every conceivable social, economic, and racial background tell me they've chosen not to have sex and have stuck by their choice.

In fact, once they make that decision, they find it's much easier to deal with the problems and temptations that come their way.

The ability to choose or decide invests us with enormous *power*—power to determine the course of our own lives, power to deal with problems, power to influence others.

However, when we make the decision to have sex—and do so knowing the dangers involved—we've surrendered that power to a physical urge that other people, including millions of teenagers, have learned to control.

Sex is certainly a strong drive. That's why every society has established rules for its control. So when we give up the power to decide whether we'll have sex, we're not only saying our glands are more powerful than our minds; but we're also saying that we're so out of control, we can't follow society's rules.

As you undoubtedly know, you can find ways to control yourself when your hormones start to rage. Here are just a few ways.

◆ If your imagination begins to focus too narrowly on sex, you can deliberately redirect your attention elsewhere. If you're watching a TV show that features erotic images and situations, you can switch to another channel. If you start to daydream about sex, grab a book on another subject and start reading. If you and friends are talking about sex in a way that encourages your worst impulses, change the subject.

◆ Physical exercise helps. I still remember a big, good-looking track star who stood up in front of his fellow students and made the following statement: "My girlfriend and I have talked about sex and have decided not to take that step until after we're married. So when we're together and things get a little out of hand—as they occasionally do— I excuse myself and take a few turns around the cinder track. Running burns up excess energy and empties me of any thoughts other than of running." When he finished, he got an ovation from the rest of the teens in the audience. It took a great deal of character for him to do that, and he earned the respect of his fellow students, who admired him for having the guts to stand up and say he wasn't "doing it." I later found out he was a track star. What incredible positives this guy had achieved in his life because of a decision he and his girlfriend made to abstain from sex until they were married! They will never have to worry about any of the negative consequences discussed in Part I. They have a lifetime of love and mutual sharing to look forward to—a win-win proposition across the board—and they haven't given up a thing!

◆ Remind yourself that you've made a commitment to abstain from sex and that if you go back on your word, you've broken a promise to yourself and have admitted that you no longer have the power to control your own life.

45

Holocaust survivor Viktor E. Frankl once said that since we have a Statue of Liberty on the East Coast of the United States, we should also have a Statue of Responsibility on the West Coast, because enjoying freedom always involves accepting responsibility.

If you have the freedom to choose between having sex and not having sex, then you also have the responsibility to make a careful and well-considered choice based on more than your own immediate pleasure.

If you're in a department store, see a pair of expensive shoes you want, and realize you can't afford them, would you consider stealing the pair of shoes? Some people would—adults as well as teenagers.

The thought might never occur to you; but if it did, you'd probably think, "I know it's wrong to steal, so I'll put the idea out of my mind. Besides, if I got caught, I'd end up in front of a judge and have a criminal record. My parents would be ashamed of me and never trust me again. And everyone at school would probably find out."

That's the way people generally make decisions about important matters.

First, they consult their conscience to see if the action they're considering is against their principles, their own code of conduct. If so, they generally reject the idea without further thought.

Second, if they don't think a principle is involved (or if they don't want to listen to the voice of conscience), then they look at how the act might affect them—their well-being, their future, their relationships with others.

Third, they think about how their action might affect those closest to them—family and friends.

And finally, they think about the impact of the action on the community and on their reputation.

In the case of stealing, most people would say that both principle and practicality send out the same message: "Don't do it."

And the same is true for many people when it comes to premarital sex: "It's wrong to have sex before marriage." And "If things go wrong, my life could be ruined."

Whatever your beliefs or principles, I urge you to make them the first order of business when you're deciding whether or not to have sex. You'll have to deal with your conscience if you make a choice that violates your own code.

Second, in making your decision about sexual involvement, consider all the private and social consequences that might occur. If necessary, make a list of potential consequences and determine whether you would like to live with pregnancy, sexually transmitted disease, the emotional shock, the hurt to your parents, and how the knowledge of your behavior might affect your reputation at school and among your friends.

When you take such matters into consideration, you're assembling the information necessary to make an informed choice about engaging in sex.

But just having all the information isn't sufficient to ensure that you will make the proper decision.

Your will also comes into play. Plenty of intelligent people who are loaded down with information make bad choices in their lives—including choices about sex. They make these mistakes because they don't have the will power to do what their reason tells them is right.

Will power is what tells you to get up rather than sleep on Saturday morning because you made a commitment to your parents to mow the lawn before lunch.

Will power is what prevents you from copying the test answers off someone else's paper when you don't know them yourself.

And will power is what you exercise when you refuse to become sexually involved because you know it would be wrong or risky or selfish.

"Exercise" is a good word to use here, because, like muscles, the will grows more powerful every time you exert it. The first time you refrain from certain pleasure, it hurts. After you refrain over and over again, you don't feel the pain any more.

But maybe you don't want to exercise your will power. Maybe you think you're ready for sex.

Before you make that decision, you need to know a little more about sex—and about yourself.

You might be wise to postpone any decision until you read the next two chapters. The first deals with the complexities of sex, and the second is a quiz—one that you can give yourself to determine whether you're ready to take this serious step and accept the consequences.

Chapter Seven

Four Dimensions of Sexual Involvement

*M*any people, maybe a majority, believe that sex is a physical act—and nothing more. That's certainly the way television, the movies, and popular music picture it.

Two people get together. They engage in a physical act. And that's all there is to it.

But that's an oversimplification of a very complicated experience. It's hard to explain all the complexities of sex, but at least we can point out a few dimensions that aren't explored in most Hollywood movies and TV sitcoms—and in some sex education courses.

Let's look at four—(1) the mental, (2) the emotional, (3) the moral, and (4) the social.

The Mental

In addition to the physical pleasure that comes from sex, people *think* about the experience, before, during, and after. Unlike animals—which couple instinctively—human beings make *judgments* about their own behavior and can decide *on the basis of reason* whether or not they engage in sexual activity.

When you don't use your reason, you often get into trouble.

For example, because your radio is acting up, in

a fit of anger you throw it out your bedroom window and it smashes on the sidewalk below.

"Why did you do such a stupid thing?" your mother asks you.

"I lost my head," you say.

"Losing your head" means failing to use your reason and, as a conse-quence, doing something foolish.

When teenagers climb into the back seat of a car, they usually leave their reason in the front seat.

When you think about the consequences of what you're about to do, you're often less likely to do it. Your desire to have brief pleasure is balanced by your weighing of the consequences if you do. Of course, sometimes pleasure is harmless—like lying back after you've finished your homework at night and listen-ing to good music.

But sometimes pleasure has its downside.

When speaking to assemblies at schools, I tell the story of what happened to me when I was in high school.

I was at an age when I came home hungry every afternoon. So I'd fix myself a snack—a peanut-butter-and-jelly sandwich, a bowl of ice cream, chips and dips, two or three candy bars. In fact, snacking on junk food became a regular afternoon habit with me.

I enjoyed every bite.

I ate more and more every day.

Soon I was snacking right up until supper time.

Then one day the basketball coach stopped me in the hallway as I was coming out of English class.

"Mike," he said, "I notice you've put on a lot of weight. Basketball practice will be starting in a couple of months. You better take off about ten or fifteen pounds or you won't be in any condition to play."

On my way home that afternoon, I thought about my predicament.

I loved my afternoon snacks. I loved basketball. I would have to make a choice between the two.

By the time I reached the house, I decided that I loved basketball more than I loved snacks, that I was going to stop snacking and maybe even cut down on what I ate at meals.

It was tough, particularly that first day. By supper time, I could have eaten a hundred candy bars. I knew I had to find something to take my mind off eating.

At this point in my assembly talk, I always ask teens what I could do to keep from thinking about food; and I always get plenty of good advice.

"You could play some basketball."

"You could do your homework."

"You could work out with weights."

"You could read a good book."

They go on and on.

The suggestions they give are all excellent—and for at least two reasons:

Each diverts my attention from my growling stomach.

And each substitutes a positive for a negative, something that builds me up instead of tearing me down.

In fact, I did all of these things; and when basketball season started, I was trim and ready to play.

My point is this: If you use your mind, you can weigh different paths to follow and figure out the right one for you.

You make rational choices where pleasure is concerned.

So there is a mental dimension to the physical act.

The Emotional

Sexuality has an emotional dimension as well—particularly for teenagers. The emotions that overtake people when they become involved in sexual activity may include, on the one hand, love and attention and caring and desire—and, on the other hand, lust, fear, disgust, rejection, self-loathing, and guilt.

Don't think that you can predict what emotions you'll feel when you choose to have sex with someone. It's a little like stepping off the front porch into a tornado; you're likely to be blown in a half dozen different directions at the same time.

So don't ignore the emotional dimension; it could be the most significant and long-lasting consequence of a decision arrived at too quickly.

The Moral

Whether you like it or not, you have to confront questions of right and wrong when you choose to have sex with someone. You may not have objections to premarital sex (though millions of people do). But you have to ask yourself what impact this decision will have on the person with whom you're involved.

And on your family.

And on his or her family.

And on your friends.

Are you taking advantage of someone?

Do you have a right to ask that person to run risks, just because you're willing to run those risks yourself?

Do you have responsibilities to your family and friends that are more important than your physical desires?

All of these are important questions that people who are about to become sexually involved need to ask themselves.

Look at it this way: Sex is either a good act or a bad act. It is never a neutral or meaningless act.

The Social

Maturity is recognizing that you're not alone in the world. You're part of a society, part of a community, and part of several smaller groups, including your family, your circle of friends, athletic teams, and clubs. And you're inevitably affected by what society and the various groups believe and want you to believe.

As I've already noted, the number one pressure on teens to have sex is peer pressure, which could also be called "social pressure." The way the group behaves often determines the way the individual behaves.

Sometimes social pressure is a good thing. For example, in part because of social pressure, we're courteous to other people and take their needs and desires into consideration.

But sometimes social pressure is a bad thing. Psychologists have found that individuals who are normally peaceful and kind can willingly participate in a lynching when they become part of a mob.

So when it comes to having sex, you have to consider the social consequences of what you're about to do.

On the one hand, a lot of teens tell you to go ahead and have sex, that everyone's doing it, that it's perfectly safe.

On the other hand, at least some of your friends and family members would strongly disapprove—and for several good reasons. So when you think about having sex, you also need to think about how your decision will affect these people and groups. (Might as well assume that if you have sex on Saturday night, somebody at school will know about it on Monday morning—and that may mean everyone, including your parents, will know about it by Thursday night.)

In considering the social dimensions of sex, the big question is this: Can you stand up to social pressure when you believe the group is wrong—and bow to social pressure when you believe the group is right?

These, then, are four aspects of sex in addition to the physical—and you shouldn't forget them in your premature rush to enjoy the physical pleasure that sex can bring.

If you try to ignore them, they'll come back to haunt you after you've already surrendered yourself to physical desire and it's too late to undo what you've done.

To put it another way: Don't sell yourself short. You're not an animal that operates strictly on the basis of physical instinct. You have a free will that is more powerful than your basic drives. Human beings make choices about their sexuality and accept responsibility for the consequences. Animals don't.

Several years ago, I bought one of the cutest female beagles I'd ever seen. Six months later, I found out just how many male dogs there were in the neighborhood. The yard was swarming with them. They'd come there by instinct.

Not one of them knocked on the back door and said, "Mr. Long, I wonder if it would be okay for Mandy to come out. I'd like to take her for a walk in the woods."

And if she'd gotten pregnant, I wouldn't have expected the dog responsible to look me straight in the eye and say, "I just want you to know that I intend to stand by Mandy and help her raise those puppies."

Also, after I'd given the puppies away, I wouldn't have expected Mandy to worry about how they were getting along or if she'd had any grandchildren yet.

Dogs are driven by instinct and have no sense of responsibility. On the other hand, you're a complicated human being with a mind, complex emotions, a moral will, and an important role to play in society.

If you give yourself this much credit, you'll have a better chance of doing the right thing when it comes to sex.

Chapter Eight

Maturity and Sex

*N*ow that we've seen how amazingly complex sex really is, I want to raise a series of questions and ask you to answer them. They can all be answered yes or no.

Don't write your answers down.

And don't take this quiz with anybody else.

You'll be grading yourself, and I want you to be as honest as you can, because this could be the most important quiz you'll ever take.

What is its purpose?

To determine whether you're mature enough to have sex.

In order to make this deter-mination, you need to consider all five of the dimensions of sex—the physical, the mental, the emotional, the moral, and the  social. If you're not mature in all of these areas, then obviously you aren't ready for sex—and that's okay.

Now, let's take a look at the questions.

Are You Physically Mature?

I'll give you the answer to this question.

If you're a teenager, you're mature enough physically, or soon will be.

Most of the body changes have already kicked in, and you're physically ready for sex—and its consequences.

If you're a boy, you can father a child.

If you're a girl, you can get pregnant.

However, the fact that you're mature physically doesn't mean that you're mature in other ways. And that's the major problem that teenagers face in a society that often urges them to go ahead and have sex as soon as they're physically ready.

Let's move on, then, to the next question.

Are You Mentally Mature?

Too many teens answer yes without ever analyzing what the question means. In order to answer intelligently, you have to ask yourself a few preliminary questions.

1 Can you understand the value of postponing imme-diate satisfaction in order to gain greater long-term benefits?

It's difficult for many people to see the long-term benefits of self-denial—and particularly hard for teenagers. Why? Because they're still in the process of discovering what to do with their lives.

Most don't know what job or business or profession they may choose.

Many don't know what additional education or training they will need.

Adulthood seems so far in the future that some don't even want to think about it, much less give up something now in preparation for the future.

That's why a lot of kids who take piano lessons would rather be watching television.

Psychologist Bill Coulson tells of a highly successful concert pianist who, when he was young, did everything he could to escape the hour-a-day practice his parents ordered. When he started his lessons, he would set the clock ahead so he'd only have to practice 50 minutes. He even persuaded a friend to put a ladder up to the window of the music room so he could climb out. (His father came home just at that moment, and he had to pretend he was climbing in.) As an adult, however, he was grateful to his parents, because he was forced to do something he wasn't mature enough to do on his own.

Highly successful musicians and athletes are the best examples of people who, at an early age, show enough maturity to postpone immediate satisfaction for long-term benefits.

Teenage musicians practice for hours while their friends hang out at the mall.

Teenage athletes diet and train while their friends stuff themselves with hamburgers and fries every afternoon.

Eventually—perhaps years later—this kind of self-denial pays off in a sold-out concert or an Olympic medal.

If you're the kind of person who's in the habit of working for long-term goals, then chances are better that you'll also be mature enough to postpone sex to ensure a bright and untroubled future.

2 *Are you dependable?*

Before you answer yes, let me ask you a couple of additional questions in order to clarify what I mean.

If I'm your parent, can I depend on you to go

where you say you're going and do what you say you're going to do? Or will I find out that you were somewhere else doing something I told you not to do?

Also, if I'm your teacher, and give you a homework assignment, can I depend on you to do all the work, do it yourself, and hand it in on time?

Think about both of these questions before you tell yourself that you're dependable.

3 Are you organized?

Is your school locker so neat that you have no trouble finding the book or paper you need?

And what about your room at home? Is the floor littered with clothes, shoes, books, audiotapes, athletic equipment, CDs, scraps of paper, tissues smeared with makeup, hair curlers, letters, empty shaving cream cans, pencils with broken points, old disposable razors, magazines, or jars of zit medicine?

And do you miss dental or medical appointments because you don't remember where you put the reminder card?

(Be honest with yourself on this one.)

4 Can you handle difficult situations intelligently— and with poise?

When you're introduced to adults are you friendly, outgoing, and courteous? Or do you shrink back, duck your head, mumble a few words, and then retreat as quickly as possible?

Are you poised enough to stand up in front of a group and express your opinion in clear, reasonable language, or do you remain in your seat, afraid to voice your opinions, even if you think they have merit?

And can you listen to praise or criticism and then respond intelligently and honestly?

5 Do you have confidence in yourself? Do you know your own strong points?

If a teacher challenges you to do something you've never done before, do you approach the task with a positive attitude or do you say, "No, I don't even want to try"?

Have you accepted the truth that without a few failures there would never be any successes? (Thomas Edison failed numerous times before he finally created a successful electric light bulb.)

Are You Emotionally Mature?

Again, you have to ask yourself a few preliminary questions before you're ready to tackle the big one.

1 Are you always in control of your feelings?

Mature people have feelings that are as strong as those of immature people. The mature ones are just able to control their emotions when the situation requires it.

For example, if you're mature, you settle differences without shouting, stomping your feet, or injuring somebody else.

You don't lose your temper.

You don't say things you'll later regret, things that will require an apology.

And speaking of apologies, are you one of those people who just can't say they're sorry when they know they've hurt someone else? Pride is one of the most dangerous of all emotions—and the first one we have to learn to control.

2 Can you face unpleasant situations without completely falling apart?

If things don't go your way—if a date falls through or you fail a test you thought you'd passed—do you cry, moan, use profanity, and throw yourself around in anguish or anger? Do you ever think or act violently?

3 Do you think you can be wholly independent and totally self-sufficient at this point in your life?

Be careful. This question is trickier than you think.

Part of being emotionally mature is knowing your own limitations. If you say, "I don't need mom or dad or school or a diploma," then you have a long way to go.

Failure to admit a dependency is self-deceiving; and an inability to stay the course until you finish high school (and perhaps even college) is short sighted and foolish. More and more, the jobs available in the work place require advanced training.

On the other hand, when you're still dependent on dad and mom for food, clothing, and shelter, do you have a right to engage in any activity that might eventually become a financial or emotional burden to them? That's why many people postpone sex and marriage until they are financially self-sufficient.

So think carefully before you answer this question.

Are You Morally Mature?

A moral person tries to help others and make the world a better place in which to live. People who do the opposite—that is, think only of themselves and have no concern for the world around them—could hardly be called moral, regardless of what else they do.

So here are some questions to ask yourself in order to determine your own moral maturity.

1 Can you accept things you can't change, and, when you can, work hard to change things for the better?
Do you try to make a difference, or do you say to yourself and others, "I don't care what happens. I'm looking out for Number One." If you have that cynical, selfish attitude, you're still a moral child and aren't ready to be involved in a serious relationship, much less one involving sex.

2 As a rule, do you put others first or do you think me, me, me?
When babies are born, they're extremely dependent—and extremely demanding. When they're hungry or need a diaper change, they don't care if mama is tired or sick or doing something important. They squall until they get what they want.

Fourteen years later, that same baby—now a teenager—should be concerned primarily with what *mama* wants or needs.

Thinking about other people rather than yourself is a sure sign of maturity—and an absolute necessity in a relationship where sex is a possibility.

3 Have you ever stopped to think if life has some deeper, larger meaning than the eye can see?
Considering such a question is a mark of moral maturity. Young people who never ask the question—who believe we're born, grow up, go to school, become

adults, and then die—are still in their moral infancy. Many remain there all their lives. But those with genuine moral sensibilities address this question in their own minds and hearts, even though they may come up with different answers.

4 *Do you set goals that invoke a higher principle than yourself?*

People who think they're the center of the universe and the ultimate judge of all right and wrong are usually just foolish—but sometimes they are dangerous. Sometimes they become dictators and rule entire nations with an iron fist.

More often they lie, cheat, steal, and murder and end up in prison or on a marble slab at the morgue.

Some are merely tyrants in their own families, telling everyone else what to do, convinced they've never made a mistake in their lives.

Most people, however, believe in a set of principles by which a society must be governed if it's to survive and prosper. Until you believe in something more powerful than you are—at the very least, an objective standard of behavior to which you can appeal—then you'll remain morally immature throughout your life.

5 *Does your behavior square with your own beliefs?*

In dealing with sexual matters, you have to assess your own beliefs and determine what you know to be right or wrong.

If you profess beliefs, then you ought to live by them. If you can't, then you're not yet mature.

So before you decide whether to have sex, you should reexamine your own beliefs and see how they square with any decision you might make.

Ask yourself this question: "If I have sex, will I do so knowing that premarital or extramarital relations go against my beliefs?"

And if so, "Do I really want to do something that I believe to be wrong?"

Are You Socially Mature?

Again, there are questions you can ask yourself to determine your social maturity.

1 Can you stand up to the crowd when you know you're right?

When the group suggests doing something you know is wrong, do you say, "Hey, wait a minute! That's not right. I have no intention of behaving that way—and neither should you."

Or do you "go along to get along"—anxious to be one of the crowd, even though you know that what the crowd is doing is dead wrong?

To put it in more specific terms, when a joint is passed around at a party, do you take a few drags—just so no one will think you're scared? Or do you refuse and leave the party before you get into trouble?

When a friend who's had too much to drink wants to drive you home, do you get into the car rather than risk an unpleasant scene, or do you refuse and try to get your friend to surrender the keys?

These are tough social situations; but if you act immaturely, you may end up either sorry or dead.

2 Can you admit to your friends when you've made a mistake and apologize when you've hurt somebody?

Immature people can't bear to admit their mistakes. When they do something wrong, they either make excuses for themselves or blame somebody else.

To admit you've made a mistake is to admit that you're human. No one gets it right every time, and other people respect and admire those who admit their shortcomings. If you haven't learned this lesson, then you haven't achieved social maturity.

3 Do you keep your promises to other people?

Keeping promises is one of the most visible signs of good character—and genuine maturity. Breaking promises is a sign of selfishness and immaturity.

Let me give you a situation so you can determine if you're a promise keeper.

You've promised Lisa that you'll drop by her house on Saturday night and help her study for the big math exam on Monday. She has trouble with math, and you've always found it easy.

Then, Saturday morning, you get a phone call from Ralph, who's very excited.

"Guess what." he tells you. "I've just won two tickets to the concert tonight. I was the 20th person to call the radio station and answer a question. So how about going with me?"

This is your favorite group. They're in town for just one night. The concert has been sold out for weeks. What a break! Then you remember Lisa.

What do you do?

Do you tell Ralph you can't go because you've promised to help Lisa study? Or do you call Lisa, make up some creative excuse, and go to the concert?

Mature people honor their promises. If you don't, then you need to do some growing up before you have sex with anyone.

This is my maturity test. Remember, however, that only you can grade yourself.

And don't feel bad if you answer no to some of these questions. Every adult has been just where you are today. Physical maturity usually takes 11–12–13 years. Mental, emotional, moral, and social maturity always takes longer. Some adults aren't there yet.

So it's okay to tell yourself you're not yet completely mature.

But it's not okay to have sex until you are.

Chapter Nine

The Love Test

*D*o you remember I told you there was a way to determine whether or not your boyfriend or girl-friend really loves you? In this chapter, I'm going to give you all the details.

First, let's look at an all-too-familiar dialogue between two teenagers who've been dating for six months. If you haven't had this conversation your-self, then you probably know someone who has.

Lamar: I really love you, Tammy, and people who love each other eventually show it by having sex. I think we've reached that point, don't you?

Tammy: I don't know. I love you too, but I'm not sure I'm ready for sex. That's such a big step.

Lamar: Not for people in love. I love you and I want you. If you really love me, you'll want me too.

Tammy: Sure I'm attracted to you. I have the same physical desires you do. It's just that I've never done this before and I'm afraid. Besides, I believe it's wrong.

Lamar: It'll be great. We're in love, aren't we?

Tammy: I do love you. Really. It's just that ...

Lamar: Look, tonight's the night. My parents are out of town. We'll have the whole house to ourselves. If you call your parents and say you're staying over at Sheila's, we can spend the entire night together. How about it? If you really love me, you'll do it.

Tammy: Well ...

Unfortunately, Tammy seems ready to call her parents, tell a lie, and spend the night with Lamar—maybe the biggest mistake of her entire life. It's obvious from this conversation that she really doesn't believe having sex is a good idea. But Lamar keeps pushing her, and she doesn't know how to answer the arguments he's offering.

He says he loves her, but does he?

I've devised a test that Tammy can use to find out whether Lamar really loves her or whether what he feels is his own selfish physical desire.

I call it the Love Test.

Here's all she has to do: Resist the pressure, give him a good reason, and then see what he says. Here  are two good reasons she could give: (1) "I don't want to get pregnant," and (2) "I just believe it's wrong to have sex before marriage."

If he loves her, he'll say, "I understand what you're

saying, and I respect your opinion. If that's the way you feel, then I won't try to pressure you any more. I love you too much to ask you to do something you don't want to do."

If he doesn't love her, he'll say, "Don't worry, you won't get pregnant. I guarantee it. We'll use a condom." Or, "What do you mean 'wrong'? It's okay if we love each other." Or, "Look, if you won't have sex with me, then we're finished."

You see, if someone is *really* in love with you, he or she wants *you* to be satisfied and happy. People in love don't think first about the gratification of their own selfish desires. They think about what's best for the person they love.

People who are merely infatuated think about themselves first —and they say and do whatever is necessary to get *their* way. They twist words. They threaten. They lie. The love test will expose them for what they are every time you use it.

It's simple, but it works. If the question of having sex comes up, you can find out if he or she loves you in a matter of seconds. Once again: Resist the pressure, give a mature reason, and then wait for the response.

If your boyfriend or girlfriend passes the love test, then you won't have to worry about the sex question ever again. The matter will be settled, and you can build a strong relationship on mutual respect and mutual understanding.

If your boyfriend or girlfriend fails the love test, at least you know where you stand. And with the knowledge that this person is self-centered and willing to take advantage of you, it's time to break off the relationship and find someone you can trust, someone who really cares about you.

It may be hard, but you'll be better off in the long run.

Chapter Ten

Red Zone

L et's assume that you didn't do very well on the maturity test and have decided to postpone sex. Does this mean you're no longer in any danger? The answer to that question depends on how firm your commitment really is.

Many teenagers have every intention of remaining virgins, yet allow themselves to engage in activities that lead them to the brink of intercourse—and one night they're so overcome with sexual desire that they break their own rule.

I realize that's a problem.

Here's how to handle it.

If you've watched football on network television, you know that announcers refer to the area inside the defense's 20-yard line as the red zone. By that, they mean the zone in which the offense is most likely to score. For the defense, the red zone means danger.

I've found this a useful concept in talking about sex. When a boy and girl go beyond a certain point in their physical relationship, they enter a red zone that exposes them to danger. Let me illustrate.

Jason and Marie are classmates in high school. They find each other very attractive, and one Saturday they decide to meet at the mall, where high school teens hang out every weekend. As they're walking around—looking in the shop windows, stopping to talk to friends—they hold hands.

No problem with that. A lot of the teens hold hands; and if either Jason or Marie goes to the mall with someone else next weekend, there's likely to be some hand-holding.

However, Jason and Marie like each other and next weekend they go to a movie. While the film is going on, Jason puts his arm around Marie. Again, no big deal. They're in a public place, and putting your arm around someone is pleasant, but not a sexually charged gesture.

As they say goodnight at Marie's front door, Jason kisses her. The kiss is a friendly peck that brushes her lips and ends up on her cheek. They are standing on Marie's steps. The porch light is on. Both kids know that Marie's parents are just inside, watching TV. The couple still hasn't reached the red zone.

However, the following Friday night, they drive out to the lake and park in a lonely spot. There, they engage in deep, intimate kissing.

They've just entered the red zone. They are involved in a highly intimate act apart from the rest of the community. Both where they are and what they're doing put them at risk. Clearly, if their emotions get out of hand, there will be nothing to stop them from having intercourse.

On Saturday night, they park in the same isolated place. They get in the back seat and begin to touch each other in intimate places, perhaps even removing some of their clothing. At this point, they have a first down on the one-yard line. They may or may not have intercourse that night, but sooner or later they'll consider it—and if they fall victim to the strong physical urge they've unleashed, both their lives could be ruined.

Note the progressive nature of their relationship. It's unlikely that they would move from holding hands at the mall to touching private parts in the back seat of a car—not all in one day. But it's easy to move gradually down the field toward the red zone. One thing leads to another—unless you consciously decide to hold the line.

Remember that it's difficult to go back once you've crossed a yard marker. Holding hands may seem too tame if you've already engaged in deep kissing. On the next date, couples generally begin with the same kind of behavior they ended up with on the previous date.

However, it's not impossible to revert to safer behavior. Many young people realize they're in the red zone and agree to return to less dangerous expressions of affection. It happens every Saturday night all over the country—and if you and your girlfriend or boyfriend have already entered the red zone, you should reexamine your relationship immediately and agree not to engage in risky behavior.

If you haven't reached the red zone yet, talk about

this problem with the person you're seeing and agree to set limits on what you do when you're alone together.

One of the most popular abstinence education programs tells teenagers not to do anything that involves the removal of a single article of clothing.

On the other hand, a prominent sex educator, who tells young people they can have sex safely if they just use a condom, has advised teenagers to engage in a number of behaviors that stop just short of having intercourse. These include intimate touching and taking off each other's clothes.

In other words, this educator advises teens to live in the red zone.

Now let me ask you this question: Which kids are more likely to have intercourse, the ones who take their clothes off or the ones who leave them on?

You know the answer to that one as well as I do.

To summarize: What you do together in the early stages of your relationship will determine whether you end up having intercourse. You should agree on limits when you first start seeing each other so that you never end up in the red zone, much less in trouble.

And by the way, setting limits isn't just the girl's responsibility. Guys are equally responsible for what happens in a relationship.

In fact, more than one guy has told me that his girlfriend is pushing him to have sex and he's having a hard time resisting the temptation.

However, girls have more to lose than guys. When birth control devices fail —as they often do—*girls* get pregnant, not guys. And girls are much more likely than guys to contract STDs through sexual intercourse.

Because they risk so much more, girls have traditionally been the ones to hold the line when the couple approaches the red zone.

But just because they may have less to lose, doesn't mean that guys have the green light to put girls at risk. A guy who really cares about a girl will want to protect her from danger—and the best way to do that is never to cross into the red zone. Remember that the moment you choose to move into the red zone you surrender the power to make right decisions. Why? Because you put reason aside and allow your feelings to take control.

The same thing happens when you use drugs or alcohol. Your power to think is impaired. Your drive for pleasure increases. Your mind is no longer in control of your body. The result—you surrender your power to choose and to make wise decisions.

I remember a conversation I had with a girl in her early teens who had been dating a guy a couple of years older than she was. We stood on the steps of the school building while she told me her story.

"Mr. Long," she said, "we'd both agreed we were too young to have sex. We'd been going together for six months, and we hadn't gone near the red zone.

"Then, one night we went to a party where everybody else was smoking dope. Our friends talked us into trying it. We both got high, but he was almost out of his mind. He took me back into a bedroom and threw himself on me.

"I tried to resist, but I was in a haze, too. I told myself, 'I love him. And if that's what he wants, then maybe I shouldn't resist any more.'

"That was the only time."

She told me this story with tears in her eyes, standing there, holding her baby in her arms.

One night, one joint, one big mistake.

You see, you lose the power to determine your own future when you use alcohol and drugs—and that power is the one thing you have going for you as a teenager. No one can take it from you. But you can throw it away by allowing your emotions to take control.

One more tip. Don't dress in such a way that you encourage others to push you toward the red zone.

I like to dress casually. If you've seen my videotape series, you'll remember that when I talk to teens, I never have on a coat and tie—only slacks and a sport shirt. More and more, Americans are "dressing down" rather than "dressing up."

But there's a limit to dressing down. If you're wearing shorts or shirts or blouses that are too tight or reveal too much of your anatomy, you're asking for trouble—whether you're a girl or a guy. That may not be fair, but it's a fact of life.

If you dress neatly and modestly, you send a message to everyone who sees you: I'm not advertising; I'm not trying to attract your attention.

That way, if someone gives you a hard time, you'll know you didn't ask for it.

In summary: Stay away from drugs. Stay away from alcohol. Stay away from sexually inviting dress. And stay away from the red zone.

Chapter Eleven

Renewed Virginity

*T*his book wasn't written just for those who have never had sex. It was also written for teens who've already had sex and want to regain control over their lives.

I know that many teenagers regret losing their virginity, but have come to believe that, since they made that first big mistake, they no longer have a good reason to abstain from sex.

That's nonsense.

First, a determination to keep your virginity is a sign that you value sex too highly to engage in it irresponsibly.

If you lose your virginity and then say to yourself and to others that you're determined hereafter to behave in a responsible manner, that means you've recovered what you lost: You value your own sexuality too highly to throw it away.

Think of that state as "renewed virginity." You're a renewed virgin because you think like a virgin again. And, more important, you behave like a virgin.

To put it another way, if you made the mistake of shoplifting an item from a local department store, would you then conclude, "Well, I've stolen once, so I guess I'll have to be a thief for the rest of my life"?

Stealing once doesn't make you a thief unless you become one in your own mind and heart.

Having sex once doesn't make you a person without sexual principles unless you choose to become one.

We all make mistakes of one sort or another; and sometimes these mistakes teach us lessons that we couldn't have learned any other way.

A lot of teenagers who have had sex once and vowed never to repeat the experience until marriage are more committed to abstinence than some virgins.

So if you've already had sex—even more than once—don't be too hard on yourself. Renew your virginity and lead a happier and healthier life. You do it right now by simply deciding you're going to change.

Listen to this teenager's story.

I'm 17, and I have been going with Lucy for almost a year. Before that I'd had sex with two other girls I was dating. We'd been going out for a month when Lucy and I had sex. It was the first time for her. The next day she called me, very upset, and told me she couldn't go out with me any more, that she was ashamed of what she'd done and that she wasn't going to do it again.

She finally agreed to talk to me at the mall, and we walked around for hours. She told me just why she thought sex before marriage was wrong, and how bad she felt about what we'd done. I told her I understood how she felt and that I was willing to date her without the sex. She said she would give it a try.

We've been going out for almost a year since that night, and we're closer than ever—mainly because I respect her for her commitment to what she believes in.

In your tapes you talk about renewed virginity. As far as I'm concerned, Lucy is a virgin again, and maybe I am too, since I'm happy the way things are.

If it worked for this couple, it can work for you— and all who are ready to be sexually responsible. Thousands of teenagers are committing themselves to renewed virginity.

Chapter Twelve

A Final Word

After all this talk about postponing sex, I have a few final words of advice and encouragement, just to remind you that where your sexuality is concerned, you are in the driver's seat.

And speaking of the driver's seat, when I'm speaking to teenagers, I always give them this problem:

"Suppose you won a brand new car in a raffle, and it was sitting in your driveway—its new paint job shining in the sun. And suppose, as you were doing your homework, your 15-year-old brother came into the room and asked to borrow your new car."

As soon as I get this far, I can see a few teens in the audience already shaking their heads and smiling. But I continue.

"Wait a minute now. Your brother has his learner's permit, and all he wants to do is drive your brand new car a mile down the highway, buy a hamburger, and come right back. Sure, his permit allows him to drive only with an adult in the car. But he only wants to go a short distance and be back within ten minutes."

By now almost all the teens in the audience are shaking their heads. But I plow on.

"You're trying to do your homework. He's driving you crazy, begging for the car—just this once. And what are the odds of his getting into trouble? Very,

very slim. Don't you realize that if you give him the keys, he'll get off your back?"

Absolutely nobody in the audience is nodding.

No one says, "Oh, the risk is worth it—just to stop him from nagging."

Everybody agrees—little brother doesn't get the car.

Why? Because even though the risk of an accident is small, if something goes wrong, it's too high a price to pay for the small amount of relief you buy when you give the kid the keys.

If audience after audience can make that choice, then they can also choose to abstain from sex for the same reason—the price you might have to pay is too high for the risk involved.

Besides, your sexuality is far more precious than that car. If you make the right choice, you'll find positive aspects to abstinence that I haven't emphasized until now—ways that help you grow mentally, emotionally, morally, and socially.

Here are just a few:

1 *People will respect you for your self-control.*

Oh, they may tell you the exact opposite and tease you or call you names; but I can assure you that when they're lying in bed at night, they will ask themselves, "What's he (or she) got in the way of inner strength and self-control that I don't have?" And, "Maybe I'm the one who's wrong about having sex. Could that be?"

You never know who among your friends or

classmates might be watching you, saying, "That person isn't going along with the crowd. Resisting the pressure to have sex takes courage. If that person has the courage, then maybe I do too."

2 If you learn to practice abstinence, you'll be able to communicate better with your boyfriend or girlfriend.

When your boyfriend or girlfriend pressures you to have sex and you resist, the next question is, "Why?" That means you'll have to give reasons. (That's the love test!)

In all likelihood, your explanation will trigger more questions, and you'll have to explain yourself in even greater detail. Such conversations help to strengthen relationships and build confidence and trust. It's important to communicate your thoughts and feelings to other people—particularly those you love.

According to studies, one of the three main reasons why marriages break down is "lack of communication." Too many married couples don't talk about important issues that divide them. They go around with unresolved conflicts bottled up inside—and then, one day, they're screaming at each other.

So you might as well learn right now to talk about such important matters—openly, frankly, and without anger. If you do, you'll learn a lot that you didn't know about other people—and about yourself as well.

3 In abstaining, you offer a priceless gift to the person you will eventually marry.

A lovely teenage girl told me not too long ago, "Mr. Long, I'm saving my virginity for my husband. Of course,

I don't even know who he is—or if I've even met him. But when I do, and I agree to marry him, I want to be able to present him with this gift—the gift of purity."

I was deeply impressed by the fact that this girl was saving herself for someone *she'd never even met*—someone she would fall in love with maybe years in the future, someone who would love her for who she was and be willing to make a lifelong commitment to her.

Wow! That relationship has got to be meaningful and permanent.

I can't believe any man or woman wouldn't be forever grateful for such a gift. And remember this: Many men and women out there would *insist* on it.

4. *Abstinence builds character.*

Character is the inner strength you create through right choices. Each time you make the right choice, you build character—and each time you make the wrong choice, you tear it down. The person who learns to postpone immediate sexual pleasure for long-term good will find that this same firmness of purpose will carry over into other aspects of life.

If you abstain from sex, you'll find it easier to abstain from alcohol and drug use.

If you don't run sexual risks, you'll be less likely to take risks by driving recklessly.

And if you put the welfare of a girlfriend or boyfriend ahead of your own in sexual matters, you're going to become more thoughtful and selfless in all your relationships.

And self-sacrifice is the foundation of good character.

$\int$*Following strict rules of conduct inspires confidence in others, including your parents.*

If you're like many teenagers, you have problems with your parents—problems of trust.

Has this dialogue ever taken place in your household shortly after dinner, just as you're slipping out the front door?

Mother (or Father):	Where are you going?
You:	Out.
Mother (or Father):	Out where?
You:	Just out.
Mother (or Father):	In which case, you're not.
You:	"Not" what?
Mother (or Father):	Not going out.

Did it ever occur to you that you could improve your relationship with your parents by following a few simple procedures?

Think about this: Your parents love you, and they know the many harmful things that can happen to young people when they're out on their own. Sexual involvement is only one possibility. Drugs and alcohol are another. So when you go "out" and don't tell your parents where you're going or what you plan to do, they worry. If you haven't already won their trust, the time has come to do just that.

Here's how.

Before you go out, always have a game plan you can pass along to your parents. Don't just plan to "hang out" with whatever friend happens to be handy. Make specific plans.

Tell your parents, "I'm going to the mall with Chris, Skinny, and Filbert. We'll be going in Filbert's car, and we'll eat dinner at the Food Court. The mall closes at 9:30. I'll be in around 10:00."

Or, "Maxine and I are going to see the movie at the Cineflex Theater. We're catching the 7:20 showing, which will be over around 10:00. Then we'll stop and get burgers. I'll drop her off and be home before 11:00."

Or, "Fred, Tameika, and I are going to rent a video and go over to Malcolm's. We'll probably fix some nachos for dinner, and I'll be in around 10:00."

Do that, stick to your game plan, and I predict you'll be able to do things you've never been allowed to do before—and with no third degree beforehand.

Why? Because your parents will see that you really aren't trying to get into trouble and will begin to trust you. You are demonstrating to them your ability to be responsible. And when you do that, watch them give you more freedom.

Why will they give you more freedom? Because you can be trusted.

In addition to telling them what you're *going* to do, also tell them what you're *not* going to do.

"Mom and dad, I'm going to a party over at Ginger's tonight. Ginger's mother will be there, and no one will be drinking."

"Mom, Shorty is picking me up and taking me to the basketball game. And no need to worry about reckless driving. He's a very careful driver."

"Dad, I know you've heard that some of the kids plan to do drugs after the prom. Don't worry. I would never do that."

Remember that your parents are worried about you because they love you. One day when you become parents of teenagers, you'll have a greater appreciation of what your parents are going through now. Show them that you love them in return by giving them less reason to worry.

These, then, are some positive aspects of choosing to abstain from sex—and there are many more. If you consider the benefits, listen to the warnings, follow helpful suggestions, and keep your wits about you, you'll have more fun during the teen years than at any other time in your life—and you'll learn the basic lessons necessary to succeed in future years—lessons in good judgment, self-control, patience, and self-lessness.

As I've said many times to teenagers, I'm optimistic about you and your generation. Young people today aren't buying the lies of the sex merchants quite as unthinkingly as the previous generation did. Teens in the 21st century have stronger ideals and stronger wills. They're more thoughtful about sex and therefore more thoughtful of each other.

For all these reasons, I'm betting that the percentage of teenagers who are sexually active will continue to decline over the next few years.

And I'm counting on you to help me win that bet.

Don't let me down.

More important, don't let yourself down. If you follow the advice in this book, I promise that you'll be glad you did for the rest of your life.

Notes

1. *Morbidity and Mortality Weekly Report,* August 14, 1998, U.S. Department of Health and Human Services, Centers for Disease Control, Vol. 47, No. SS-3.
2. Kaiser Family Foundation, *Sex and the Mass Media,* September 1995.
3. *The Tulsa World,* October 17, 1995.
4. Michael Medved, *Hollywood vs. America: Popular Culture and the War on Traditional Values.*
5. "A Portrait of Adolescence," Institute for Youth Development, p. 32.
6. U.S. Department of Education, "Will Safe 'Sex Education' Prevent AIDS?" 1988.
7. Allan Parachini, *Los Angeles Times,* January 27, 1988.
8. For example, Margaret Fischl, et al., "Heterosexual Transmission of Human Immunodeficiency Virus (HIV): Relationship of Sexual Practices to Seroconversion," III International Conference on AIDS, June 1–5, 1987, Abstracts Volume, p. 178.
9. Kaiser Family Foundation, *National Survey of Teens: Teens Talk about Dating, Intimacy, and Their Sexual Experiences,* 1998.

Teens love the brand new "Everyone Is NOT Doing It" T-Shirt

A great way for teens to take a stand on abstinence and insure dialogue at home with parents is wearing the brand new **"Everyone Is NOT Doing It"** T-Shirt. Designed on a "cool" ash color for teens, these quality shirts get attention. Designer Mike Long explained why he made the shirt the way he did at a recent parent/teen conference he conducted in Grand Junction, Colorado.

"These kids love this style shirt. It's the 'in thing!' We put the logo from our **'Everyone Is NOT Doing It'** videotape series that is currently being shown in over 4000 school systems and youth organizations nationwide on the front. When a kid wears this shirt and friends or parents see the logo, the first question they will ask is: 'What is everyone NOT doing?' This allows the teen wearing the shirt to explain. It gets dialogue going like never before. Then the teen can show a friend or parent exactly where he or she stands on the issue because on the back of the shirt is printed the words: RESPECT. RESPONSIBILITY. CHARACTER."

Available in Medium, Large, and Extra-Large: $16.95 plus $2.95 s/h. Reduced prices for bulk orders of 10 or more, please call toll free 1-866-645-3566. For more information, please see our web site at www.mikelong.com.

M.L. Video Productions, Inc.   **CALL TOLL FREE**
P.O. Box 61863   **1-866-MIKELONG**
Durham, NC, **27715-1863.**   (1-866-645-3566)

☐ T-shirt $16.95 + $2.95 shipping/handling

Please send me _____T-shirt(s), size(s) _____.

Enclosed is my check for $_____ or charge my ☐ Mastercard ☐ Visa:

No. _____Exp Date _____

Signature_____

Name _____

Address _____

City_____State_____Zip_____

North Carolina residents please add 6% sales tax to total order. Please allow two weeks for delivery.

Mike Long is available to speak in your area

3-day visit: **The most productive way to promote abstinence education in your community**
In-service training for teachers, Community Awareness programs for parents, School Assemblies for teens
All in one visit!!!

There is no better way to utilize federal Abstinence Education funds than to secure Mike Long for a 3 day visit to your area.

On **Day 1** Mr. Long provides an in-service training for teachers, health professionals, youth leaders, etc. The in-service consists of 3 sessions (appr.1½ hrs. each). Typically, two sessions take place in the morning, break for lunch, then complete the training with session 3 in the early afternoon. "Teachers and youth leaders come away from my trainings highly motivated to put these new abstinence teaching strategies to work in the classroom," Long said. "They learn for the first time that teaching abstinence is not telling kids to 'Just say NO.' It is teaching teens responsibility, discipline, and maturity in a fun way that builds their character."

Day 2 of Mr. Long's visit consists of 2 assembly programs in area schools and a Community Awareness Program in the evening. "School board members, administrators, clergy, community leaders, and concerned parents are always convinced that this directive educational strategy is exactly what needs to be taught to teens," Long said. "The Community Awareness Program eliminates all the fallacies and confusion they have about abstinence and is very convincing to them that this is the way to go."

Day 3 consists of more school assemblies for teens. "The beautiful thing about conducting this 3 day event in an area is teachers are trained how to effectively teach abstinence in the classroom and they can't wait to begin. Administrators are convinced that this is the way to go. Parents learn these directive educational techniques. Teens are highly motivated from assemblies. Then teachers and parents can follow-up using the '**Everyone Is NOT Doing It**' series," Long said. "It is a beautiful way to coordinate a unified effort between the local organization, school system, parents, and community. It's win, win across the board!"

For more information about this incredible 3-day package or how to bring Mike Long to your area to conduct your abstinence education programs and trainings, contact him at toll free at 1-866-645-3566.

Parents: Everyone Is NOT Doing It

Effectively Teaching Teenagers Abstinence

Mike Long

Foreword by Coach Dean Smith

If you are a parent, teacher, or youth leader who wants the best for your kids, Mike Long's book is for you! Mike will show you how to get on your teenagers' level about sex, drugs, alcohol, and violence. You'll learn how to direct them in making smart, healthy decisions that build character, responsibility, maturity, and discipline. Mike's "directive teaching" style WORKS because, rather than give orders and lay down laws, you'll direct teenagers to make the right decisions on their own.

This book will help you become the kind of director your teenager so desperately needs. The doors of communication will burst open in a way you never thought possible, and you will be able to help your child lead a happier, healthier, and more fulfilling life.

Moral instruction has been the responsibility of parents since the beginning of history. It is best done authoritatively. Mike Long has presented in his book a simple method of authoritatively teaching sex

See next page

to preteens and teens. More importantly the principles he espouses are applicable to all moral instruction. This book is a must for all parents who earnestly desire to provide their children values that will help them avoid the pain that arises out of immorality.

—William P. Wilson, M.D., Professor Emeritus of Psychiatry,
Duke University Medical Center, Durham, North Carolina

Becoming NASCAR racing champions requires much work and dedication. As grandparents and parents, it takes even more time and effort to keep our kids on the right track. Mike Long's book is a timely resource that will make our job much easier in directing the lives of our preteens and teens, especially during these times of incredible peer pressure. We highly recommend it.

—Ned & Dale Jarrett, NASCAR Winston Cup Champions

Per Copy $16.95 plus $2.95 s/h

Reduced prices for bulk orders of 10 copies or more, call toll free
866-645-3566. For more information, please see our Web site at
www.mikelong.com. Order from:

M.L. Video Productions, Inc.   **CALL TOLL FREE**
P.O. Box 61863,   **1-866-MIKELONG**
Durham, NC, 27715-1863.   (1-866-645-3566)

☐ *Parents: Everyone is NOT Doing It: Effectively Teaching Teenagers Abstinence* $16.95 + $2.95 s/h

Please send me ____ copies of *Parents: Everyone is NOT Doing it*. Enclosed is

my check for $_____ or charge my   ☐ Mastercard   ☐ Visa:

No. _____Exp Date_____

Signature _____

Name_____

Address _____

City_____State____Zip _____

North Carolina residents please add 6% sales tax to total order. Please allow two weeks for delivery.